# The Fantastic Flying Squirrel

Written and photographed
by Nic Bishop

It is night in the forest.
Many animals are asleep but
some are waking up.

A flying squirrel wakes up in her tree den.

The flying squirrel is hungry and
she's looking for food.
What can she see?

The flying squirrel jumps.

The flying squirrel glides.

She finds some acorns. **Crunch, crunch.**

She's still
hungry and
she wants
more food.

Shhhh!
What can
she hear?

A grasshopper is crunching on a leaf.

A hungry owl hears the grasshopper too.

The flying squirrel jumps.

The flying squirrel glides.

She finds the grasshopper first!
**Crunch, crunch.**

The flying squirrel goes back to her den and climbs inside.

She isn't hungry any more.

# What does the flying squirrel do?

she climbs

she looks

she listens

she jumps

she glides

she eats

# 🐾 Ideas for guided reading 🐾

**Learning objectives:** Understand that a line of writing is not necessarily the same as a sentence; predict what a given book might be about from the covers; using awareness of grammar to decipher new or unfamiliar words; blend sounds to read words with consonant clusters in initial and final position; speaking to describe incidents in an audible voice.

**Curriculum links:** Science: light and dark, sound and hearing

**Interest words:** flying, squirrel, forest, animals, hungry, glides, acorns, crunch, grasshopper, climbs, listens

**High frequency words:** but, some, up, her, and, looking, what, wants, too, any, more

**Word count:** 128

## Getting started

- Before showing the book, explain to the children that they are going to be reading an information book. Tell them that you already know what the book is about although you haven't read it. Ask them how you know (from the cover).

- Show the book and ask them to look at the cover and then each predict one thing the book might tell them. Ensure that all the children can read the title accurately.

- Turn to pp2-3 and discuss the pictures, drawing out key words *night*, *forest*, *wakes*. Which sentence tells them that the flying squirrel is awake?

- Walk through the book together up to p15, and discuss what is happening in the pictures. Remind them to look at consonant clusters to help solve words like *glides* and *crunch*.

## Reading and responding

- Ask the children, as they read, to write down on a whiteboard three or more things a flying squirrel does. They could draw, write or remember these.